Neuschwanstein Castle

Official guide

Revised by
Uwe Gerd Schatz
and
Friederike Ulrichs

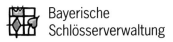

Bayerische
Schlösserverwaltung

Contents

Following pages: Upper Courtyard: on the left is the Palas, on the right the Connecting Building with the Knights' House in the middle; the windows are in the Romanesque style.

One of three majolica swans made for Neuschwanstein Castle by Villeroy & Boch, 1884. The body is hollow and was used as a container for plants and flowers.

Design for the window arcades on the first floor of the Knights' House by the scene painter Christian Jank, 1870, with naturalistic plants and animals from a programme by Hyazinth Holland; the trees are representations of the World Ash Tree Yggdrasil, the roots of which were home to the dwarf-like Nibelungen.

»Idea«

Ludwig II announced his plan to build »New Hohenschwangau Castle«, which was only called »Neuschwanstein« after his death, in the following letter dated 13 May 1868 to his friend Richard Wagner: »It is my intention to rebuild the old castle ruin of Hohenschwangau near the Pöllat Gorge in the authentic style of the old German knights' castles ... The location is one of the most beautiful one could find, holy and unapproachable, a worthy temple for the divine friend who has brought salvation and true blessing to the world. It will also remind you of Tannhäuser (Singers' Hall with a view of the castle in the background) and Lohengrin (castle courtyard, open corridor, path to the chapel); this castle will be in every way more beautiful and habitable than Hohenschwangau further down, which is desecrated every year by the prose of my mother; they will take revenge, the desecrated gods, and come to live with Us on the lofty heights, breathing the air of heaven«.

Design for the window arcades on the first floor of the Knights' House by the architect Julius Hofmann, 1884, with abstract plants and animals

Plan of 1820 with views and ground plans of the ruins Hinter- and Vorderhohenschwangau over which Neuschwanstein Castle was built;

After the disappointments and setbacks early on in his reign, the king increasingly withdrew from public life to the seclusion of the mountains he loved so much. It was here, in the area he had known since he was a child, that he decided to build a new residence. His father Maximilian II had acquired Schwanstein, the seat of the knights of Schwangau, in 1832 when he was still crown prince, with the idea of »restoring [the ruin] to its original medi-

on the right Hohenschwangau Castle with the ground plan

eval form«. The result was the present Hohenschwangau Castle, built from plans by the set-designer Domenico Quaglio. Maximilian II ordered the construction of paths and lookout points in the area around Hohenschwangau to enable him to enjoy the scenery, and also had the iron bridge, the »Marienbrücke«, built above the Pöllat Gorge for his consort Marie. In 1855 he made plans to build a viewing pavilion on a narrow ridge high above this gorge, which commanded a magnificent view of the whole area and was originally the location of the medieval castle Vorderhohenschwangau. This never progressed beyond the planning stage. In 1867 Ludwig II decided to »rebuild« Vorderhohenschwangau as his castle. In the building documents of 1868 the project was still called »Restoration of the old ruined castle«, although what was left of the medieval building was eventually removed to make way for the new building.

SWAN KNIGHT

In Neuschwanstein the late romantic concept of restoration, which makes a further appearance in 1883 in Ludwig's plans for Falkenstein Castle, is combined with the idea of a new castle of the swan knight Lohengrin. The knight's heraldic animal, the swan, had already featured as a leitmotif in the castle built by Ludwig's father, a building which had had a substantial influence on the development of Ludwig's artistic tastes. The swan was also the historic heraldic animal of the knights of Schwangau. Maximilian saw himself as their successor and adopted their coat of arms. His son followed suit, and the swan thus also features as a heraldic animal in Neuschwanstein; it is sometimes used in combination with the medieval coat of arms of the Pfalzgraf bei Rhein, a title still held by Ludwig, and the lozengy of the royal coat-of-arms of Bavaria. Ludwig II had been familiar with the Lohengrin legend since he was a child from the murals of his father's castle. He was introduced to Wagner's »Lohengrin« on 2 February 1861 in the Munich Court Opera House and was captivated. Thus, in the course of time, Ludwig II came to see himself in typically romantic fashion as both a real knight of Schwangau and the fictitious swan knight Lohengrin, while always remaining fully conscious of himself as the ruling king of Bavaria.

The scene painter Christian Jank, who produced the first drawings for Neuschwanstein, clearly based the castle courtyard on the stage set of the 2nd act of the opera »Lohengrin«, »Courtyard of Antwerp Castle« as designed by Angelo II Quaglio for the Munich Lohengrin production of 1867. A reference to Act 3 in the form of a bedroom resembling the bridal chamber for Elsa and Lohengrin was to be incorporated in the Bower. However, as shown by the letter to Wagner quoted above, the king visualized Neuschwanstein not only as Lohengrin's castle, but also as Tannhäuser's. Ludwig was involved in the preparation of a new production of »Tannhäuser« and, at Wagner's suggestion, went on 31 May 1867

Richard Wagner.
Photograph by
Pierre Petit &
Trinquart, Paris
1860

Right side:
King Ludwig II
in civilian attire.
Photograph by
Joseph Albert,
March 1867

to visit the scene of the historic Singers' Contest, the Wartburg. A prime example of the tendency in Germany to romanticize all things medieval, this castle had been »reconstructed« in the same year. For Ludwig it represented an authentic combination of the Middle Ages and the artistic celebration of minnesong and knighthood which prevailed in this era. It was exactly this combination he was aiming for, and the romantically »reconstructed« Wartburg gave him ideas as to how he might achieve it. From the beginning the Neuschwanstein project included a Singers' Hall modelled on the Banqueting Hall of the Wartburg, although the latter was not com-

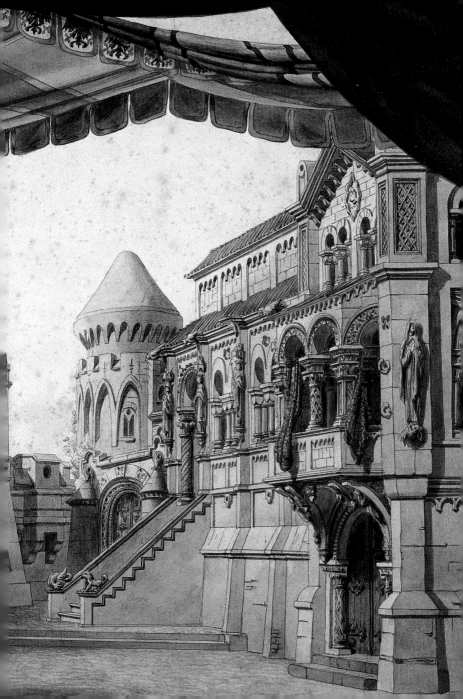

pleted until 1876. In 1858 King Friedrich Wilhelm IV of Prussia expressly ordered the plans for this Wartburg hall to be used for the set of Act 2 in the first Berlin production of »Tannhäuser«. Ludwig had a new Singers' Hall constructed for Neuschwanstein which was designed by Jank and was a combination of the Festival Hall and the Singers' Bower of the medieval Singers' Hall in the Wartburg. The Neuschwanstein Singers' Hall also became the model for subsequent »Tannhäuser« sets. The building which combined all the scenes from »Lohengrin« and »Tannhäuser« would not of course have been complete without the »Grotto in the Hörselberg«. From 1880 the room next to Ludwig II's study was transformed into a small artificial grotto with a waterfall by a landscape sculptor, or scenic sculptor in modern theatre terminology. As a result of his lifelong fascination with Wagner's work, Ludwig II was always a very generous patron of the 19th century's leading music dramatist. The premières of »Tristan und Isolde«, »Die Meistersinger von Nürnberg«, »Rheingold« and »Walküre« also had epoch-making sets due to the very high standards set by Ludwig, and for a short period from 1865 to 1870 Munich as a result became the music capital of Europe. Without Ludwig II, neither Wagner's late works nor the Bayreuth festival would ever have come into being. Ludwig II was personally involved in the composition of Wagner's last work for the stage, »Parsifal«: in the final years of his life he identified himself with this figure, and he was also regarded in this light by Wagner, a fact of which Ludwig was aware. This explains the mural programme of the Singers' Hall and its function as a monument.

ROMANESQUE AND ROMANTIC

The government architect selected to convert Christian Jank's pictorial representations into plans was Eduard

Riedel, who had already redesigned Berg Palace for Ludwig's father in 1849–51. In accordance with the king's wishes, Jank turned the »robber knight's castle« with late gothic elements that he had originally designed into a monumental »Romanesque« castle with a five-storey Palas in the general style of the Wartburg Palas. Neuschwanstein, which everyone now oddly enough thinks of as a typical »medieval castle«, is thus not a copy of any existing building, but a characteristic example of historicism, in which architectural motifs from the Wartburg are combined with those of castles from medieval book illustrations. It is significant that Jank's project was criticized for not being faithful to history. The painter Michael Welter, who was recommended to the king by the castellan of Wartburg for his historical accuracy, undertook to provide the »necessary details« for Neuschwanstein based on Romanesque examples and declared that Jank's final designs would »incite the most virulent and bitter criticism«. Court secretary Düfflipp turned down Welter's proposals in a letter of 21 November 1871, for the following most revealing reasons: »It is the will of His Majesty the King that the new castle be built in the Romanesque style. We are now living in the year 1871, centuries after the period of the Romanesque style, and there can be no doubt that the achievements that have since been attained in the areas of art and science will also benefit us in the construction of this building. – By this I do not in the least mean that we should alter the style itself in a way that would impair its character, but neither do I mean that we should recreate the old days in every respect and not benefit from experience which would have been made use of them, had it been available«. Historicism frequently involved not just copying the historical styles, but »perfecting« them using all the latest craft skills and technical means. For this reason the typical combination of modern (building) technology and historic architectural and furnishing styles was

Ideal design for
Neuschwanstein
Castle by
Christian Jank
in 1868, which
incorporated
Richard Wagner's
instructions for
the set of Act 2
of the opera
Lohengrin;
east view of the
Upper Courtyard,
with the keep
and chapel
in the centre

by no means considered a contradiction. This was also Ludwig II's philosophy, so that the »Romanesque« castle of Neuschwanstein has a very modern kitchen, hot air heating, and numerous large, tightly-fitting windows with frames made of industrial steel.

The exterior of the castle became increasingly austere when Georg Dollmann succeeded Riedel in 1874 and many of the picturesque details in Jank's designs were dropped. In the sections completed in simplified form after 1886 this tendency increased.

Mural »Lohengrin's arrival« (in Brabant) by August von Heckel, 1880/81, in the salon

Julius Hofmann, who completed the complex on the basis of Riedel's plans from 1886 to 1892, designed the entire »Romanesque« interior of Neuschwanstein complete with furnishing in accordance with the king's ideas. Only the bedroom, designed by Peter Herwegen, and the adjacent chapel are in late-gothic style with furniture that is comparatively historic by comparison with the Biedermeier neo-gothic interiors of Hohenschwangau.

MURALS

The king checked every detail of the interior from the drafts and frequently ordered corrections to be made before work could begin. He was particularly involved with the planning of the murals. His father had similarly decorated Hohenschwangau with murals of local legends, some of them from sketches by Moritz von Schwind. Ludwig II consulted the literary historian Dr. Hyazinth Holland, a specialist in medieval iconography, who provided him with a wide variety of possible themes, but the motifs he chose for the castle were almost exclusively related to Wagner's music dramas. However, in 1879 he had already decreed that »the pictures in the new castle should be based on the original legends and not on Wagner's interpretation of them«. It was thus Ludwig's conscious wish to go back to the historic sources of Wagner's

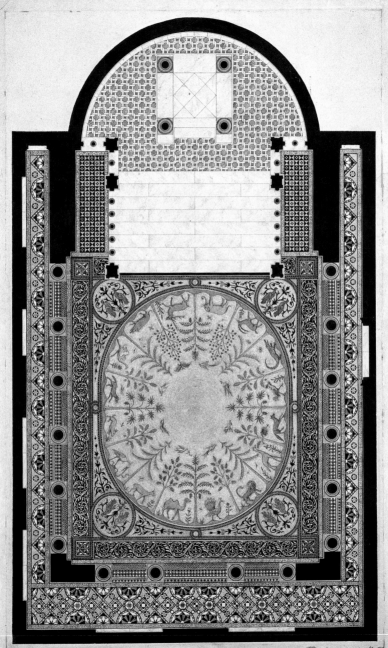

J Hoffmann

work. For this he wanted »only painters who make an exact study of the medieval poetry«, in other words painters of historical scenes, who kept strictly to the concept derived by the king from his literary studies and based on the principle of poetic glorification of a real or imagined historical truth. This was however no different from what was generally expected of the specialized painters of historical scenes throughout the 19th century.

THRONE HALL

Even later on in the proceedings, the whole Neuschwanstein programme frequently had to be altered as the king's concept of it changed. Years before the premiere in Bayreuth, he was already studying the stage set for Wagner's »Parsifal« and in 1876 he asked Eduard Ille to design him a Grail Hall in Byzantine style, based on Hagia Sophia in Constantinople. From this he developed the idea of a Throne Hall in Neuschwanstein. In the final design for this room, by Julius Hofmann, which was only completed in 1881 and also incorporated medieval descriptions of the legendary Grail Hall, the »Wartburg« designed for the young king was transformed into Parsifal's »Castle of the Holy Grail«. The six canonized kings featured in the apse, whose deeds are depicted in the hall's murals, represented Ludwig II's idea of pure kingship »by the Grace of God«. The figures beneath the cupola representing the pre-Christian cultures and realms of India, Rome, Greece, Persia and Egypt and »The moral code of the Old Testament« on the opposite wall symbolize the secular and sacred basis of the Christian kingdom. On the floor is a mosaic of concentrically ordered animals and plants which shows that Ludwig II, who designed the complex programme of the hall himself, was also well versed in Buddhist and Oriental philosophy. In the cupola directly above the life cycle on the floor is the sun, indicating that kingship is part of a cos-

Mosaic on the floor of the Throne Hall with plants and animals, coloured pen-and-ink drawing by Julius Hofmann, 1883; the mosaic produced by Anton Detoma in 1885/87 is almost identical.

Following pages: South view of the Throne Hall with chandelier in the form of a crown by Eduard Wollenweber, columns with coloured stucco-work, ornamental painting and murals on a gold background, 1885/86

Julius Hofmann (1840–1896)

The architect Julius Hofmann trained in Vienna. In 1864 he worked for Maximilian, Archduke of Austria and Emperor of Mexico. From 1867 on he was employed in the service of Ludwig II, first as a colleague of Georg Dollmann, and from 1884 as court architect.

Hofmann was in charge of building Neuschwanstein, and also drew up plans for the interior of every room in the castle, which other artists and their workshops were commissioned to produce. The extremely versatile Hofmann designed not only the furniture, textiles, murals and sculptures, but everything down to the washstand set in the king's bedroom and the glass paintings in the windows. As a typical representative of historicism he based his work on historic styles, with a preference for the Romanesque and gothic eras, while also including elements of non-European architecture taken from Chinese pavilions and Arabic mosques.

Hofmann's designs also confirm him in many respects as a forerunner and pioneer of art nouveau.

Design for the throne canopy (not constructed) in the Throne Hall; on the upholstered back of the throne is the monogram of Ludwig II. Coloured pen-and-ink drawing by Julius Hofmann, 1884

mological whole. This room, which was not merely a throne hall but rather a temple to kingship, sums up Ludwig II's complex view of the world. In addition to this, however, this unique cult centre and monument to kingship also incorporates the dynasty of the ruling king of Bavaria: Ludwig II expressly requested the inclusion of clear references to the All Saints Church in the Munich Residence, built in the Byzantine style by his grandfather Ludwig I from 1826. The composition of the apse painting was taken from another of Ludwig I's churches, St Bonifaz in Munich, in which he is buried.

The original programme was changed and the Singers' Hall was now designed to prepare the way for the Throne Hall; in 1883–84 it was decorated with murals presenting the Parzival saga according to Wolfram von Eschenbach. In the Singers' Bower Parzival appears as the King of the Holy Grail, and the opposite wall shows his son Lohengrin departing from the Castle of the Holy Grail. The picture programme thus comes full circle and links up with the swan knight theme which was the starting point of Neuschwanstein.

HISTORICISM AND THE MODERN AGE

The Throne Hall of Neuschwanstein, which was to have been completed in the year of Ludwig II's death and never had its throne, is the only one of the king's Byzantine projects that was ever completed. Two large Byzantine palaces were designed for him, first in 1869 by Georg Dollmann and again towards the end of his life in 1885 by Julius Hofmann, which were intended to manifest his kingship by God's grace, as was also the very different palace of Herrenchiemsee. Both were to have been built in the Graswangtal near Lin-

Three-legged candelabra in the Throne Hall with Romanesque and Art Nouveau elements, designed by Julius Hofmann in 1884 and made by Eduard Wollenweber in gilt brass with Bohemian glass stones

27

derhof Palace. Since Falkenstein Castle near Pfronten also never progressed beyond the planning stage, Neuschwanstein remained in many respects a unique monument to one of the greatest builders from the House of Wittelsbach, whose works are also different because of their relationship to the theatre. At the same time, as a main work of historicism Neuschwanstein also underlines the unmistakable achievements of 19th-century art, with, for example, the surprisingly early manifestations of art nouveau in Jank's architectural features or in details of Hofmann's interior such as the »Romanesque« chandeliers of the Throne Hall. In addition the very latest technology was used, such as the steel construction for the Throne Hall and the multicoloured electric lighting in the grotto, often only being incorporated for the purpose of illusion. For the king however, his palaces and castles – which by contrast with most royal buildings were not intended for the public – were more than an illusion, more than an imaginary world into which he withdrew out of protest against a bourgeois world that did not understand him. They were his life and a setting in which history was to be resurrected – just as it was on the stage of his court theatre. Ludwig II, who by no means ruined the state financially with his projects, as is often maintained, but paid for everything out of his own pocket, applied himself to these undertakings with great skill and an energy which he often lacked in political matters. When foreign creditor banks forced him to stop building by threatening to seize his property, life lost its purpose for the king, who made his last journey from Neuschwanstein to Berg on 12 June 1886 after being declared insane. Thus the king, who could not cope with the role of a monarch in a constitutional monarchy, and was called the »only true king of this century« by Paul Verlaine in a sonnet of 1886, finally perished because, with a lack of compromise shown by none of his contemporaries, he created an alternative world in which he could live as the absolutist or medieval king of Bavaria.

Planning history

In 1867 Ludwig II collected numerous ideas for the buildings he was planning. While he was making a study of Versailles, he also asked to be shown round Pierrefond Castle, which the famous architect Viollet-le-Duc had only recently »reconstructed« in medieval style. Viollet's encyclopaedic publications on historic styles were a further source of ideas for Ludwig II's Neuschwanstein. The Festival Hall and Singers' Hall of the Wartburg were a fixed part of the programme from start to finish, while other rooms were dropped from the plans or substantially altered.

The architect Eduard Riedel was instructed by Ludwig II to make drawings of the Wartburg, while Christian Jank produced drawings of the Romanesque ornamentation. The architect and artist worked closely together. Riedel dealt with the practical architectural aspects of Ludwig's historically-oriented specifications, such as the structural engineering, development and functions. Jank then turned the plans into picturesque views, since the king, who was a very visual person, always wanted to know exactly what his buildings were going to look like. The first drafts of the new castle are predominantly influenced by the Wartburg, but have been adapted to the existing foundations of the two medieval ruins: here the two main buildings, the Palas and the keep (a separate construction), stand one behind the other. The palace chapel was to be located on the ground floor of the keep. The plans were then soon expanded as the king elaborated on his original ideas and new building sections were added: the Knights' House on the north side, the Bower on the south side and the Gateway Building on the east side, as well as an increasing number of towers. The

Preliminary design for Neuschwanstein from 1868 by Christian Jank; based on the two ruined castles on the site, it is much smaller than the final building.

Schnitt

nach

A – B.

Maßstab:
1 : 100

zur Erbauung eines Lustschlosses des
Königlichen Baurath
zu
Hohenschwangau – s

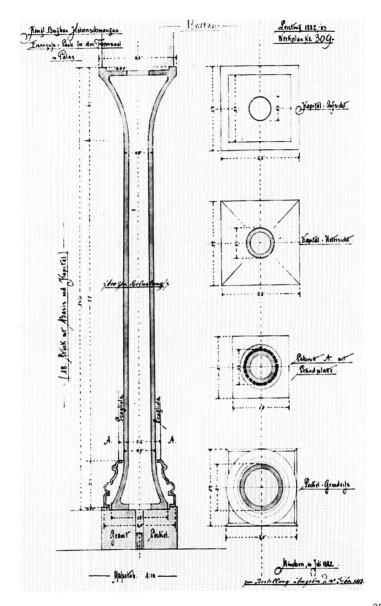

1886

Exterior

The castle complex occupies a narrow, 1008-metre ridge with steep sides and a backdrop of rugged mountain scenery. It consists of the Gateway Building at the eastern end, the Bower to the south, the Knights' House with the Square Tower to the north and the Palas with two towers at the western end. With the exception of the Gateway Building, the exterior is clad with white limestone, making it visible for miles around.

South view of Neuschwanstein Castle from the Marien-Brücke; from left to right: Palas, Bower, Square Tower and Gateway Building

NORTHERN FAÇADE (FROM THE FINAL BEND OF THE ACCESS ROAD)

From left to right: north corner tower of the Gateway Building, Lower Connecting Building, Square Tower, Upper Connecting Building, Knight's House with staircase tower, north façade of the eastern Palas section with Conservatory, rectangular staircase tower with statue of the Madonna, study balcony, octagonal staircase tower (65 m) with statue of St George and north façade of the Throne Hall tract. All the exterior statues are by Philipp Perron.

WESTERN FAÇADE (FROM THE PATH TO THE MARIENBRÜCKE)

The western façade ends in a gable with two square corner turrets, which is crowned with a copper-embossed statue of a knight. On the northwestern corner is a stone statue of St Cecilia. Two-storey balcony in front of the Throne Hall with arcades on masked consoles. The door on the ground floor was originally intended to lead onto a terrace, but this was never constructed.

SOUTHERN FAÇADE (FROM THE MARIENBRÜCKE)

Upper Courtyard with Bower, Knights' House and Palas; the foundations of the castle chapel that was never built are visible on the ground.

Impressive view of the castle complex across the precipitous Pöllat Gorge, with the flat countryside surrounding the town of Füssen beyond. From left to right: Palas with round staircase tower and the oriel and balcony of the bedroom, Bower with square staircase tower and octagonal projection, square tower of the Knight's House, southern corner tower of the Gateway Building. A crevasse with bridged by the foundations of the castle can be seen below the Bower.

EASTERN FAÇADE (VISITORS' ENTRANCE; SEE COVER PICTURE)

Two-storey, crenellated Gateway Building with round corner towers and a three-storey middle section with a crow-stepped gable. The towers and the projecting gate section are clad with white limestone, the middle section with decorative bricks and Molasse sandstone. Over the gateway is the Bavarian royal coat of arms, above which is a gallery with two balcony-like corner projections.

LOWER COURTYARD

On the east side is the Gateway Building, on the north side the Connecting Building with an outside staircase to the Gateway Building and Square Tower, on the west side a wall with pillars and a fountain and an outside staircase leading to the Upper Courtyard, on the south side a low wall facing the Pöllat Gorge.
Entrance hall of the Gateway Building with groined vault; on the portal of the guards' room the relief of a dog

with the circumscription »Fidelity is vigilant day and night«. Courtyard façade clad with white limestone and yellowish Rhaetic sandstone. On the second floor is a balcony with colonnades. The rooms on this floor, which are not accessible, served as provisional accommodation for the king while the Palas apartments were under construction; in the rooms on the first floor the government commission which was to declare Ludwig II unfit to govern was for a short time held captive.

The 45-metre Square Tower ends with a projecting gallery and a cylindrical, crenellated top section.

The projecting section of the wall was originally intended as the foundation of the choir in the palace chapel that was to have been located on the ground floor of the keep; the keep, however, was never built.

UPPER COURTYARD

Embossed copper lion on the east gable of the Palas, with a symmetrical mane in medieval style

On the west side is the gable façade of the Palas, on the south side the Bower, on the east side the low parapet of the wall, on the north side the Connecting Building with the Knights' House. The foundation walls of the keep are marked out on the ground.

An outside staircase leads up to the main portal of the Palas on the first floor. Façade with two-storey oriels; above the balcony of the Singers' Hall are two frescoes, »St George« and »Patrona Bavariae«, by Wilhelm Hauschild; gable crowned by a copper-embossed lion.

The Bower was only completed in its present form in 1892. According to the 1885 plans, the façade

was to have ornamental sculpture and statues of female saints. Central projection with portal and balcony. On the west side an outside staircase leading to the first floor.

In the middle of the two-storey Connecting Building between the Palas and the Square Tower is the three-storey Knights' House with a gable. The building has the same windows, modelled on the Wartburg, as the rest of the castle; it was completed without the naturalistic ornamentation originally planned for the first floor.

Console busts in late medieval style under the balcony oriel of the Palas

Rooms

Pages above:
Throne Hall with
apse; mural of
Christ as ruler
of the world with
Mary and John
the Baptist, be-
neath them
between palm
trees six canon-
ized kings

On the first floor of the so-called Palas (the residential part of a medieval castle) are the servants' quarters, with authentic furnishings. The rooms in the Palas are accessed via the two staircase towers in the northwest and southeast. The rooms on the second floor were never finished and are today used for administrative purposes.

The apartments and state rooms of the king are on the third and fourth floors and the interiors were more or less complete by 1886. All the rooms are dominated by paintings, which cover the walls and ceilings and include elements taken from Persian and medieval book illustration, and decorative carving. Every detail of the interior was designed by Julius Hofmann (see box p. 26), and produced by other artists and workshops. The imposing chandeliers and candelabras of gilt brass in the Throne Room, the Singers' Hall and the king's apartments are from Eduard Wollenweber's workshop, and the elaborate door fittings are by Karl Moradelli. Max Steinmetz produced the magnificently embroidered textiles.

1 LOWER HALL

The Palas consists of two sections, which meet at an obtuse angle due to the limitations of the ridge-top site. The hall, connecting the two parts, thus narrows at one end. Marble portals open into the Throne Room on the west side and the royal apartments on the opposite side. On the walls are illustrations of the Sigurd saga from the Old Norse saga »Edda«, a collection of sagas, songs and sayings. Sigurd corresponds to the Siegfried of the Middle High German Nibelungenlied.

Murals of the Sigurd legend by Wilhelm Hauschild, Karl Schultheiß, Josef Munsch and Ferdinand Piloty (1882/83). The brothers Fafnir and Regin are in possession of a hoard of golden treasure, the Nibelungen treasure, on which, however, the gods have laid a curse. Fafnir seizes the treasure for himself and turns himself into a dragon to guard it. Regin forges the beautiful sword Gram and gives it to the young king Sigurd, who uses it to kill Fafnir but then also Regin, and thus acquires the fateful treasure. (»Gripyn prophesies Sigurd's fate« ▪ »Regin forges the sword Gram for Sigurd« »Sigurd kills Fafnir«). Sigurd finds the sleeping Valkyrie Brynhild confined within a ring of fire and pledges to be true to her. Continuing on his journey, he reaches the kingdom of Franconia on the Rhine. The king's daughter Gudrun gives him a magic potion which makes him forget Brynhild and marry her instead. (»Sigurd rides through the raging fire to Brynhild« ▪ »Gudrun gives Sigurd the potion«). Now Gudrun's broth-

Door fittings decorated with leaves and tendrils and handles in the form of swans' heads by Karl Moradelli

er Gunnar wants to win Brynhild. He can only do this with Sigurd's help, and Brynhild demands atonement for the humiliation she has suffered at Sigurd's hands. The youngest of Gudrun's brothers, Guttorm, is forced to kill Sigurd. Brynhild kills herself with the sword and is burned with Sigurd on the same pyre. (»Sigurd's death« ■ »Gudrun awaits Sigurd's return« ■ »Brynhild scorns Gunnar« ■ »Gudrun's lament over Sigurd's body« ■ »Sigurd and Brynhild are burned together on the same pyre«).

Painted, wrought-iron chandelier with swan motif by Karl Moradelli.

Mural in the Lower Hall illustrating the Sigurd-legend: »Gudrun's lament over Sigurd's body«, 1882/83

2 THRONE HALL

This sumptuous, church-like hall with its massive, four-metre high chandelier occupies the third and fourth floors and the entire west section of the Palas.
The Throne Hall was inspired by Byzantine churches and in particular the All Saints Court Church in Munich. In the northern apse there was to be a throne in place of the altar, but this was never constructed after the death of the king. This combination of church and throne room illustrates Ludwig's interpretation of kingship: he saw himself not just as a king by God's grace, but also as a mediator between God and the whole world. This idea is also expressed in the cupola, which is decorated with stars, and the floor mosaic beneath it, which shows the earth with its plants and animals. Beneath the cupola are representatives of pre-Christian kingdoms. The pictures in the apse area show Christ, the Twelve Apostles and six holy kings, while the deeds of the kings and other saints are illustrated on the walls. The Throne Hall was not intended for state occasions. It is an expression of Ludwig's expectations of kingship.

Murals by Wilhelm Hauschild, Waldemar Kolmsperger and other artists. In the apse: »Christ in his glory, with John and Mary, symbols of the Evangelists and angels«; beneath these figures are six canonized kings: »Kasimir of Poland« ■ »Stephen I of Hungary« ■ »Emperor Heinrich II« ■ »Louis IX of France« ■ »Ferdinand III of Spain« ■ »Edward the Confessor of England«; next to the throne steps: »The Twelve Apostles«. In the arcades: »King Edward of England as a righteous knight« ■ »King Ferdinand of Spain fighting the Moors« ■ »St George« (in the background the silhouette of Falkenstein Castle near Pfronten, which Ludwig II planned to build within sight of Neuschwanstein) ■ »Landgravine Elisabeth von Thüringen performing charitable works« ■ »Queen Clothilde of France converts her husband to Christianity«. On the gallery: »Conversion of the Hungarians by King Stephen of Hungary« ■ »Emperor Heinrich II as a founder of churches« ■ »St Michael« ■ »King Louis IX of France as a benefactor«. Under the vault: »Ancient law« ■ »The moral law of the Old Testament«.

Mural in the Throne Hall: »St George killing the dragon« by Waldemar Kolmsperger, 1884, with the silhouette of Falkenstein Castle, which Ludwig II also planned to build, in the background

▨3 ANTEROOM

The apartments of Ludwig II are entered through the oak-panelled anteroom on the third floor. An electric bell system was installed in 1885 so that the servant on duty here could be summoned from any other room.

▨4 DINING ROOM

Wolfram von Eschenbach and other minnesingers feature in the dining room murals, which are framed with oak panelling decorated with bas-relief carvings. On the dining table is a centrepiece in marble and gilt bronze, which shows Siegfried fighting the dragon. As in all the king's rooms, the textiles are very elaborate; here they are made of red silk with gold embroidery and trimmings.

Murals by Ferdinand Piloty and Josef Aigner: »Landgrave Hermann presents gifts to minstrels« ■ »Gottfried von Straßburg«

Following pages: View of the dining room with the original furnishings (historical photograph); today the table has been moved to the side to create a passage through the room.

51

■ »Heinrich von Veldeke's poem Äneïde is returned to him by the Landgrave after its rediscovery« ■ »The sorcerer Klingsor, disguised as an oriental merchant, sets the court riddles to solve« ■ »Wolfram von Eschenbach« ■ »Singers' Contest at the Wartburg« ■ »The sorcerer Klingsor brings Heinrich von Ofterdingen to the Wartburg« ■ »Reinmar von Zweter« ■ »The Landgrave commissions Wolfram von Eschenbach to translate the poem ›Willehalm‹ « ■ »Performance by minstrels at the Landgrave's court«. In the quatrefoils above the window arches: »Prudence and Temperance« ■ »Justice and Valour«.

Centrepiece by Eduard Wollenweber from a model by Ludwig Bierling, 1885/86.

5 **BEDROOM**

As in all the residences of Ludwig II, the king's bedroom is particularly sumptuous. The leitmotif is the legend of Tristan and Isolde, and the two main characters feature not only in the murals, but also in the carvings on the door and the ceramic figures on the tiled stove. The state bed in the neo-gothic style and the seat coverings are in blue silk, with embroidered and appliquéd lions, swans, crowns, lilies and the Bavarian coat of arms. One of the most unusual features is the washstand, with a fountain in the form of a silver-plated swan. Small swans also decorate the washstand set – water jug, sponge and soap containers – which was designed by Eduard Wollenweber.

Murals of the Tristan legend by August Spieß (1881): Tristan travels to Ireland to win the hand of the beautiful Isolde for King Marke of Cornwall. On their way back Tristan drinks a goblet of wine with Isolde which, unknown to them, is a love potion (»Tristan gives Isolde the love potion«). The lovers meet secretly in the garden of the castle in Cornwall, although Isolde is now married to King Marke. Here Marke takes them by surprise and

Centrepiece in gilt bronze: »Siegfried fighting the dragon«, designed by Ludwig Bierling for the dining room table and made by Eduard Wollenweber, 1885/86

Following pages: Bedroom with murals of Tristan und Isolde, oak furniture and carvings by Anton Pössenbacher, washstand with silver-plated swan fountain designed by Julius Hofmann

Madonna, 1883, modelled on a figure in Hagia Sophia, bed headboard, Andreas Müller

Right side: Armchair with baldachin and reading table in a style resembling that of a medieval prie-dieu; view from the window of the Pollät Gorge with the Marien-brücke

Tristan is seriously injured by Marke's liegeman Melot in a duel (»Tristan bids farewell to Isolde« ■ »Tristan and Isolde in the garden of the Cornwall castle«). Kurwenal brings the dying Tristan to Kareol, to the castle of his fathers. King Marke learns that a magic potion was the cause of his wife's unfaithfulness and travels to Kareol to forgive the lovers. But it is too late: Tristan dies of his injuries and Isolde of grief (»Tristan waiting for Isolde« ■ »Isolde's arrival with Kurwenal« ■ »Tristan and Isolde united in death«). ■ »Lady reading Tristan« ■ »Faithfulness« ■ »Love«. All the oak furniture in the room is by Anton Pössenbacher, 1883.

The oratory adjacent to the bedroom is also in the neo-gothic style. The murals, glass windows and the middle picture on the altar feature Louis IX of France, the patron saint of the king. There was a further connection between Ludwig II and the ruling Bourbon family: King Louis XVI – a direct descendant of Louis IX – was the godfather of his grandfather King Ludwig I.

Oratory, with walls, altar and glass windows decorated with pictures of St Louis, the patron saint of Ludwig II

Painting on the winged altar and murals by Wilhelm Hauschild: »St Louis« ■ »The death of Tristan, the son of St Louis« ■ »St Louis receives the Banner of the Cross«.

Glass painting from the Mayer'sche Hofkunstanstalt (1882): »St Louis receiving extreme unction«.

Ivory crucifix by Anton Dießl, 1883.

7 DRESSING ROOM

The dressing room is decorated in the style of a garden hall with an illusionistic ceiling painting of a garden bower with a trellis of vines open to the sky. The murals between the panelling show scenes from the life and poems of Walther von der Vogelweide (ca. 1170–1230) and Hans Sachs (1494–1576). Above the arch leading to the oriel recess are half-length portraits of both poets. The seat covers and the curtains are made of violet silk magnificently embroidered in gold with an elaborate design of leaves, tendrils and pairs of peacocks. In the oriel recess is the king's jewelry box.

Murals by Eduard Ille (pupil of Moritz von Schwind): »The birds teach Walther von der Vogelweide how to sing« ■ »Walther sings his song in praise of German morals at the court of Duke Guelph« ■ »Walther wins the support of the German princes for

the crusade« ■ »Walther on his journeys« ■ »I sat on a rock ...«
■ »Walther participating in a crusade« ■ »Under the linden-
tree...« ■ »Hans Sachs performing a song to an audience that in-
cludes Pirkheimer, Peter Vischer and Dürer« ■ »Sachs presenting a young singer with the master's chain« ■ »Sachs with his
friends« ■ »Sachs in his study«.

8 **SALON**

The L-shaped salon has an alcove furnished with chairs
and separated from the rest of the room by columns. The
large oak cupboard is modelled on an item of furniture
from the Wartburg and is decorated with scenes from

*Right side:
Dressing room
with illusionistic
ceiling painting
and murals of
scenes from the
lives and poems
of Walther von
der Vogelweide
and Hans Sachs*

*Ludwig II's jewel
casket with a
painting of a
medieval theme,
»Droit du
seigneur«, in the
oriel recess of
the dressing
room, 1884/86*

*Following pages:
Salon with al-
cove, murals of
the Lohengrin
legend and blue
silk textiles em-
broidered with
swans and lilies*

medieval poems. The murals in this room show scenes from the Lohengrin saga, which Ludwig II identified with in particular on account of the Grail Knight theme and the swan motif. The swan was also Ludwig's heraldic animal as a Knight of Schwangau. As in the bedroom, the curtains and coverings are made of blue silk and embroidered with swans and lilies. There is also a container for plants or flowers in the form of a large majolica swan by Villeroy & Boch.

Murals of the Lohengrin saga by Wilhelm Hauschild and August von Heckel: The Knight Lohengrin is selected through the miracle of the Grail to protect the king's daughter Elsa (»Miracle of the Grail« ■ »Lohengrin's arrival« ■ »Elsa tells Lohengrin her troubles«). In a duel he defeats Count Telramund, who has accused Elsa of fratricide and wants to become king himself (»Elsa asks Lohengrin for his support« ■ »Lohengrin lands at Antwerp« ■ »The mass before the duel« ■ »Arrival of the contestants« ■ »Duel with Telramund«). Elsa and Lohengrin marry, although she knows nothing about his origins and must never ask. After they are married, Elsa nevertheless asks Lohengrin the fateful question. The swan which brought Lohengrin then reappears and changes into Elsa's missing brother. Lohengrin, however, must return to the Castle of the Holy Grail (»Lohengrin weds Elsa« ■ »Elsa goes to the cathedral« ■ »Elsa's question« ■ »Transformation of the swan«).

Pictures on the cupboard doors by Ferdinand Piloty: »Gottfried von Straßburg with lady and monk« ■ »Wolfram von Eschenbach presents his Parzival poem to the Landgrave of Thüringen« ■ »The legendary blind poet of the Nibelungenlied with Bishop Pilgrim and scribe«.

9 **GROTTO AND CONSERVATORY**

Between the salon and the study is a room that would not normally be found in a royal apartment: a small grotto. The

Artificial grotto by August Dirigl with coloured lighting, a reproduction of the Hörselberg (or Venus Mountain) from the Tannhäuser legend

Writing desk, chairs, stool and writing set with Lohengrin sculpture in the study by Philipp Perron and Ferdinand Harrach, 1883 (historical photograph)

Right side: Study with murals of the Tannhäuser legend; like all the rooms of the royal apartments, it has an elaborately carved and painted ceiling.

set-designer August Dirigl created the artificial dripstone cave, which originally had coloured lighting and a waterfall. It was based on the idea of the Hörselberg in the Tannhäuser saga. The adjacent glassed-in balcony housed the king's conservatory; the small fountain was intended for a Moorish Hall, which was not however completed.

10 STUDY

The murals show the Tannhäuser saga. As in the opera of the same name, this is linked with the Singers' Contest on the Wartburg. The king worked at the large table in the centre of the room, on which his writing set still stands. The cupboard was used to store the castle plans and drafts of Neuschwanstein. Elaborate carvings cover the beams and consoles of the ceiling.

Murals of the Tannhäuser saga by Josef Aigner: The itinerant knight and singer Tannhäuser falls in love with Elisabeth, niece of the Landgrave of Thüringen. Since the differences in their so-

cial status prevent them from ever marrying, he travels on in despair (»Tannhäuser playing for dancers«). Heedless of the warnings he receives, he enters the Hörselberg where the goddess Venus resides and for a year enjoys the pleasures of her realm (»Tannhäuser is warned by the faithful Eckhart« ■ »Tannhäuser in the Venus grotto«). However, he then grows weary of the goddess, leaves the Hörselberg and arrives once again at the Wartburg, where a Singers' Contest is taking place (»Shepherd boy playing a shawn in front of the Wartburg« ■ »Tannhäuser meets the Landgrave« ■ »Tannhäuser goes to the Wartburg« ■ Tannhäuser's arrival at the Wartburg ■ »Landgravine Elisabeth« ■ »Singers' Contest at the Wartburg«). Tannhäuser shocks the singers by singing in praise of sensual love. He is banned from the Wartburg, repents of his sins and goes on a pilgrimage to Rome to ask the Pope's forgiveness. This is refused him, and he returns to Venus' enchanted mountain (»Tannhäuser as a penitent before Pope Urban IV« ■ »Tannhäuser's return to Venus' enchanted mountain«). Murals of medieval rulers: »Duke Friedrich the Valiant of Austria« ■ »Duke Otto the Illustrious of Landshut«.

⓫ ANTEROOM

The oak-panelled anteroom or adjutant room is furnished with a table, chairs and a tiled stove, as well as a couch for the use of the servant waiting on the king at night. As in the study, the room is divided by two arches and pillars.

⓬ PASSAGE

⓭ UPPER HALL

From the upper hall on the fourth floor a marble portal on the west side leads to the gallery of the Throne Hall and two marble portals on the east side lead into the

Singers' Hall. The murals illustrate the Gudrun saga from the Old Norse Edda, the continuation of the Sigurd saga (see Room 1).

Murals of the Gudrun saga by Wilhelm Hauschild (1883/84): Gudrun corresponds to Kriemhild in the Nibelungen saga. After Sigurd's death she lives in solitude, but then marries Atli (Attila), king of the Huns (»Gudrun goes to reside with Thora after Sigurd's death« ▪ »Gudrun embroidering the heroic deeds of her ancestors with Thora« ▪ »Atli woos Gudrun« ▪ »Gudrun's bridal journey with Atli«). In order to gain possession of the Nibelungen treasure, Atli invites Gudrun's brothers to his court. In the battle for the treasure, the Nibelungs are killed (»Atli tells Gudrun his dreams« ▪ »Atli's messengers at the court of Gunnar« ▪ »The battle between the Nibelungs and the Huns«). Gudrun

Anteroom for the footman on duty, decorated more simply than the king's apartments

»Gudrun greeting her brothers«, mural illustrating the Gudrun legend in the Upper Hall by Wilhelm Hauschild, 1883/84, ceiling painting and marble portal with Bavarian lion and swan coat of arms designed by Julius Hofmann

avenges them by stabbing Atli in his sleep and setting fire to the hall where the king's followers are sleeping. She tries to end her life by leaping into the sea but is borne on the waves to the coast of King Jonakur's realm. (»Gudrun holds a funeral repast for the warriors« ■ »Gunnar fettered in the castle tower« ■ »Gudrun throws the torch into the castle« ■ »Gudrun borne alive to distant shores«).

14 SINGERS' HALL

The Singers' Hall was one of the king's favourite projects and next to the Throne Hall the most important room in the castle. It occupies the whole of the fourth floor in the eastern section of the Palas and is a combination of two historical rooms in the Wartburg – the Festival Hall and the Singers' Hall. The Singers' Hall in the Wartburg was allegedly the location of the famous Singers' Contest which is also featured in Richard Wagner's opera »Tannhäuser«. In 1867 Ludwig II went at Wagner's suggestion to look at the Wartburg.

On the short, western side is the Singers' Bower, separated from the rest of the room by steps and three arcades, and with a small gallery above it. The murals in the hall do not however deal primarily with the Singers' Contest but with the saga of Parzival and the Holy Grail (see box). The bower, which resembles a stage, is painted with a forest scene – the sacred forest that surrounds the Castle of the Holy Grail. Parzival's son is the »Swan Knight« Lohengrin, with whom the picture cycle ends. Depicted on the high coffered ceiling are the signs of the zodiac.

Like the Throne Hall, this hall was also never used for large banquets or musical performances: it was Ludwig's monument to the knights and legends of medieval times. Tannhäuser, Parzival and Lohengrin were the figures with whom the king had identified since his youth.

Running along the long, north side is a gallery, with Flayetanis and Kyot, the authors or translators of the Grail saga, depicted on the consoles. Behind the retaining wall of the gallery is a passage with a coloured coffered ceiling painted with scrolls bearing the names of minnesingers. On the opposite, window wall, the ceiling consoles are carved with figures and symbols connected with the Parzival legend such as the winged Lucifer, who during his fall lost a precious stone from his crown, from which the Holy Grail was later made.

Murals of the Parzival saga in the hall by August Spieß (1883/84): On the window wall: »Parzival's first encounter with

Following pages: Singers' Hall with Singers' Bower and gallery, murals illustrating the Parzival legend, chandeliers and candelabras of gilt brass

The Parzival saga

Queen Herzeloide brings up her son in isolation after the death of her consort Gamuret. However, after his first encounter with knights, he departs for the legendary court of King Arthur. Here Parzival meets the King of Cumberland, the »Red Knight«, whom he kills with his boy's spear. With the knight's armour he survives further adventures and he then marries Queen Kondwiramur. On

»Parzival fighting the Red Knight«, mural in the Singers' Hall by August Spieß, 1883/84

the way to visit his mother Parzival is received by the ailing king Amfortas at the Castle of the Holy Grail, Montsalvat, and at the banquet he sees the miraculous Grail. The knights hope that Parzival will release Amfortas from his suffering but Parzival fails to ask the king the crucial question about his health. That night Parzival is tortured by

nightmares and the following day he is scornfully dismissed from the castle. He roams restlessly from country to country; one Good Friday morning the hermit Trevrezent reveals to him the secret of the Grail. Continuing on his travels he encounters Gawan, the strongest of Arthur's knights, and defeats him without recognizing him. With the help of the sorceress Kundrie, Parzival finds his way back to the Castle of the Holy Grail, Montsalvat, where his wife Kondwiramur and their son Lohengrin are waiting for him. In Montsalvat he releases Amfortas by asking him sympathetically about his health and becomes King of the Holy Grail.

Right: »Parzival at the court of Amfortas« (Castle of the Holy Grail), mural in the Singers' Hall by August Spieß, 1883/84

Castle kitchen with the latest technology of the day: a free-standing stove with an underground smoke outlet, a built-in oven, a sideboard and cupboards for keeping the food warm

knighthood« ■ »Parzival taking leave of Herzeloide« ■ »Parzival's fight with the Red Knight« ■ »Parzival weds Kondwiramur« ■ »Parzival meets Amfortas«. In the quatrefoils above: »Repane and Feirefiz« ■ »Sigune and Schianatulander« ■ »Ginover and Artus« ■ »Herzeloide and Gamuret«. In the alcove: »Truth« ■ »Wisdom«. On the wall opposite the Singers' Bower: »Parzival at Amfortas' court« ■ »Parzival scorned by the castle guard« ■ »Parzival waited on by women« ■ »Parzival's dream«. On the gallery wall: »Kundrie summons Parzival« ■ »Parzival meets his half brother Feirefiz« ■ »Parzival visits the hermit Trevrezent« ■ »Kundrie's flight«. Above the entrance the royal Bavarian coat of arms: »Ludovicus II. rex.bavar.

com.palat.« (Ludwig II, King of Bavaria, Count Palatinate). On the bower tondos with pictures of »Kardeiz« ■ »Lohengrin« ■ »Elsa« ■ »Prester John«, in the corner spandrels: »Parzival as Grail King« ■ »Lohengrin leaves the Castle of the Holy Grail«. On the side walls of the Bower: »Frau Minne« ■ »Walther von der Vogelweide« ■ »Heinrich von Ofterdingen« ■ »Klingsor« ■ »Tree of Knowledge« ■ »Faith« ■ »Wolfram von Eschenbach« ■ »Scriber and Biterolf« ■ »Reimar von Zweter« ■ »The triumph of faith«.

Murals of events leading up to the story of Parzival in the gallery passage by August Spieß, Josef Munsch, Ferdinand Piloty and Waldemar Kolmsperger the Elder: »Gamuret in the Moorish town of Patelamunt« ■ »Gamuret wins Herzeloide's hand and crown« ■ »Constancy« ■ »Faithfulness« ■ »Gawan bringing about the reconciliation and engagement of Melianze and Obie« ■ »Gawan saves a wounded man« ■ »Temperance«. ■ In the oriel recess: »Justice« ■ »Fortitude«. On the window wall: »Gawan's fight with the lion at Klingsor's enchanted castle« ■ »Gawan breaks a branch from the tree of King Gramoflanz« ■ »Gawan and Orgeluse's wedding celebration« ■ »Gamuret's victory over Belakane's enemies« ■ »Bliss«. In the anteroom: »Parzival meets pilgrims on Good Friday« (the king ordered this picture to be completed on Good Friday 1884).

KITCHEN

The kitchen was equipped with the latest technology of the day. It included a large stove and a sideboard, a large and a small spit, a built-in roasting oven with a plate warmer, a baking oven, a mortar and a fish tank. Adjacent to it are the pantry, with a built-in crockery cupboard and glass-partitioned room for the chef-de-cuisine, and the scullery.

Figure on p. 83: King Ludwig II of Bavaria in general's uniform and coronation mantle. Painting by Ferdinand Piloty the Younger, 1865, in the King Ludwig II Museum, Royal Palace of Herrenchiemsee

NEO-ROMANESQUE TILED STOVE
ON THE GROUND FLOOR

Right: Design
(not realized)
dating from
1880 for the
west wall of the
salon; on the
left the door, on
the right the
tiled stove in
front of a
mural. Indian
ink, water-
colour, signed
»J. Hofmann«

Stove made
of coloured
glazed tiles,
signed and
dated inside
»Mittermayr
München
28/8/1880«;
height
410 cm

The architect Julius Hofmann had designed three elaborately decorated tiled stoves for the residential rooms in the
Palas, adapted to the style of the rooms: »Gothic« for the
bedroom, »Romanesque« for the dressing room and the
salon. They were all completed and delivered in
1880/81 by the Munich stove setter Joseph Xaver
Mittermayr, but Ludwig was only satisfied with
the unostentatious brown stove for the bedroom; the two colourfully glazed »Romanesque« stoves were stored without
ever having been used and much lower,
simpler stoves were installed instead.
This tiled stove is typical of the 19th century with respect to its size, but is built
like a tower with a square pedestal and
elaborate late Romanesque architectural ornamentation (jagged style) and
crowned with a lantern dome. Round the
octagonal middle section, matching the
theme of the salon (Lohengrin, the
Knight of the Holy Grail) are plaques
with the words »Fides« (faith), »Caritas«
(love) and »Spes« (hope); the figures
representing the cardinal Christian
virtues, which can be seen on Hofmann's design and were intended to
go in the columned arcades beneath the plaques, have not been
preserved. This stove is a good example of the inventiveness and
creativity of historicism: there are
no Romanesque forerunners for a
design of this kind.

14.   1.

81

Biographical data of King Ludwig II

His grandfather was King Ludwig I (reigned 1825–1848) who gave Munich a new status as a centre of the arts in Europe with monumental buildings and new collections. His son Maximilian II (reigned 1848–1864) married Princess Marie of Prussia, who was the mother of Ludwig II and Otto, in 1842.

1845 25 August: Ludwig II is born in Nymphenburg Palace near Munich, on the name day and birthday of his grandfather Ludwig I.

1861 2 February: Crown Prince Ludwig sees Richard Wagner's romantic opera »Lohengrin« for the first time.

1864 10 March: Death of Maximilian II; Ludwig II becomes king.
4 May: First meeting of the king with Richard Wagner.

1865 10 June: Premiere of »Tristan und Isolde« in the Munich Hof- and Nationaltheater.

1866 Bavaria loses the so-called »Bruderkrieg« against Prussia: from then on Ludwig II is no longer sovereign; this is a major catastrophe in his life and the main reason for his retreat from the realities of his position as a constitutional monarch.

1867 22 January: Engagement to Sophie, Duchess in Bavaria, sister of Empress Elisabeth of Austria.
31 May: Journey to the Wartburg, resulting in important ideas acquired for a new castle of his own.
20 July: Journey to Paris with his grandfather Ludwig I:
visit to the World Exhibition in Paris and Versailles Palace.
He studies the palace with his Versailles project in mind and visits Pierrefonds Palace to obtain ideas for his new castle.
10 October: The engagement is broken off.

Linderhof Palace (above),
The Great Hall of mirrors in the Royal Palace of Herrenchiemsee (right)

1868 21 June: Premiere of »Die Meistersinger von Nürnberg« in the Munich Hof- and Nationaltheater.
First drafts of Neuschwanstein Castle and the Versailles project.

1869 Drafts of a Byzantine palace and Linderhof Palace.
5 September: The foundation stone of Neuschwanstein is laid.
22 September: »Das Rheingold« by Richard Wagner is first performed in the Munich Hof- and Nationaltheater.

1870 26 June: Premiere of »Die Walküre« in the Munich Hof- and Nationaltheater.
Prussia's war with France: Bavaria is forced to fight on the side of Prussia.

1871 Victory over France; the Prussian king becomes German emperor; Ludwig acknowledges him and in this way acquires certain independent rights for his subject state of Bavaria. From then on he concentrates on the development of his alternative world.

1872 6 May: First of a total of 209 »private shows«, theatre and opera performances for Ludwig II alone, most of them in the Hoftheater.
22 May: The foundation stone of the Festival Theatre in Bayreuth is laid.

1873 Purchase of the Herreninsel in the Chiemsee.

1874 Journey to Paris and Versailles; Ludwig studies the palace for his Versailles project.

1876 6–9 August and 27–31 August: Visit to the first Bayreuth Festival, dress rehearsal and third performance of »Der Ring des Nibelungen«.

1878 21 May: The foundation stone of the New Palace of Herrenchiemsee is laid.

1879 Completion of Linderhof Palace.

The new dress coach of King Ludwig II, 1870/71, Marstallmuseum in Nymphenburg Palace (above)

King Ludwig II in civilian attire, photo by Joseph Albert, ca. 1885 (right side)

1883 to 1886   Drafts of Falkenstein Castle, a Byzantine palace and a Chinese summer palace.
Increasing financial difficulties.

1886   10 June: Ludwig II is certified insane and his uncle Prince Luitpold of Bavaria takes over the regency for Ludwig's incurably ill younger brother.
12 June: Ludwig II is arrested in Neuschwanstein Castle and interned in Berg Palace on Lake Starnberg.
13 June: Ludwig II dies in Lake Starnberg, together with the psychiatrist who certified him insane.
19 June: King Ludwig II of Bavaria is laid to rest in the crypt of St Michael's Church in Munich.

Index of artists and craftsmen

Further Literature

W. RICHTER: Ludwig II., König von Bayern. München 11. Aufl. 1985 (1. Aufl. 1939).

H. KREISEL: Die Schlösser Ludwigs II. von Bayern. Darmstadt 1955.

D. and M. PETZET: Die Richard-Wagner-Bühne König Ludwigs II. München 1970.

R. HACKER: Ludwig II. von Bayern in Augenzeugenberichten. München 1972 ff.

S. RUSS: Die Ikonographie der Wandmalereien in Schloß Neuschwanstein. Diss. Heidelberg 1974.

J. TSCHOEKE: Neuschwanstein. Planungs- und Baugeschichte eines königlichen Burgbaus im ausgehenden 19. Jahrhundert. Diss. München 1975.

G. BAUMGARTNER: Königliche Träume. Ludwig II. und seine Bauten. München 1981.

H. G. EVERS: Ludwig II. Theaterfürst, König, Bauherr. München 1986.

E. HANSLIK und J. WAGNER: Ludwig II. König von Bayern (1845–1886). Internationale Bibliographie zu Leben und Wirkung. Frankfurt/Main 1986.

G. HOJER (Hg.): König Ludwig II.-Museum Herrenchiemsee. Katalog. München 1986.

L. HÜTTL: Ludwig II., König von Bayern. Eine Biographie. München 1986.

E. D. SCHMID: König Ludwig II. im Portrait. München 1996.

M. SPANGENBERG: Der Thronsaal von Schloß Neuschwanstein. König Ludwig II. und sein Verständnis vom Gottesgnadentum. Also available in English (The Throne Room in Schloss Neuschwanstein. Ludwig II of Bavaria and his vision of Divine Right). Regensburg 1999.

J. L. SCHLIM: Ludwig II. Traum und Technik. München 2001 u. 2010.

A. SCHICK: Möbel für den Märchenkönig. Ludwig II. und die Münchner Hofschreinerei Anton Pössenbacher. Furniture for the Dream King. Ludwig II and the Munich Court Cabinet-Maker Anton Pössenbacher (in German and English). Stuttgart 2003.

Picture book for children: P. O. KRÜCKMANN: Der König und sein Schloss Neuschwanstein. München 2001.

Neuschwanstein Plans

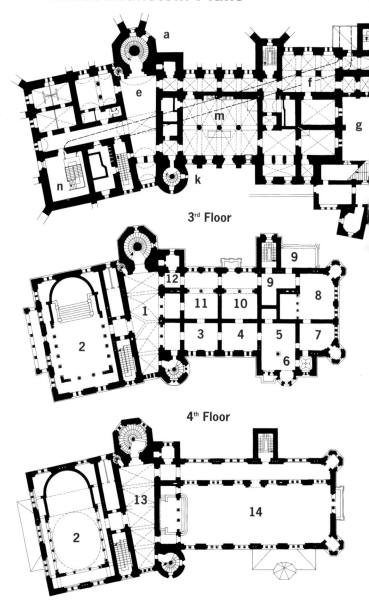

3rd Floor

4th Floor

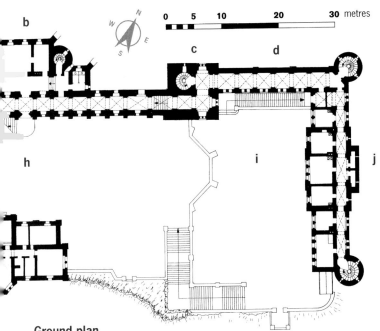

PLACES OF INTEREST ADMINISTERED BY THE BAVARIAN PALACE DEPARTMENT

www.schloesser.bayern.de

INFORMATION

Ansbach ■ Residence of the Margraves of Ansbach
Early rococo state apartments, collection of Ansbach faience and porcelain, Court Garden with orangery
TEL. (09 81) 95 38 39 - 0 · **FAX** (09 81) 95 38 39 - 40

Aschaffenburg ■ Johannisburg Palace
Art gallery and electoral apartments, collection of cork models, Palace Garden, Municipal Palace Museum
TEL. (0 60 21) 3 86 57 - 0 · **FAX** (0 60 21) 3 86 57 - 16

■ Pompeiianum
Replica of a Roman villa and Antiquities Museum

■ Schönbusch Palace and Park
Small neoclassical palace in an English landscape garden

Bamberg ■ New Residence in Bamberg
Imperial Hall and baroque state rooms, art gallery, Rose Garden
TEL. (09 51) 5 19 39 - 0 and 5 19 39 - 114
FAX (09 51) 5 19 39 - 129

Bamberg/ ■ Seehof Palace
Memmelsdorf Residential and state rooms, rococo garden, cascade with waterworks
TEL. (09 51) 40 95 - 70 · **FAX** (09 51) 40 95 - 72

Bayreuth ■ New Palace
Margravial residence in the Bayreuth Rococo style with the Wilhelmine Museum, the Museum of Bayreuth Faience, Court Garden with orangery
TEL. (09 21) 7 59 69 - 21 · **FAX** (09 21) 7 59 69 - 15

■ Margravial Opera House

Bayreuth/ ■ Museum of Garden Design Fantaisie Palace and Park
Donndorf **TEL.** (09 21) 73 14 00 - 11 · **FAX** (09 21) 73 14 00 - 18

Bayreuth/ ■ Hermitage Old Palace
Hermitage Margravine Wilhelmine's rooms, grotto, historic gardens with waterworks
TEL. (09 21) 7 59 69 - 37 · **FAX** (09 21) 7 59 69 - 41

Burg Lauenstein
Ludwigsstadt

Schloss Rosenau
Coburg
Veste Coburg
Schloss Ehrenburg
Kulmbach
Plassenburg

72

Burg Zwernitz
Felsengarten Sanspareil

Neue Residenz Bamberg
70
Bayreuth
Schloss Eremitage
Markgräfliches Opernhaus

Schloss Seehof
Bamberg
Schloss Fantaisie
Neues Schloss Bayreuth

schaffenburg
npejanum
Schloss Johannisburg

loss
önbusch
Würzburg

Schloss Veitshöchheim
Residenz Würzburg

Alte Hofhaltung

73

9

Festung Marienberg

Schnaittach

Festung Rothenberg

Cadolzburg
Nürnberg

93

Tucherschlösschen

Kaiserburg Nürnberg

6

Residenz Ansbach
Ansbach

6

3

Residenz Ellingen
Weißenburg

Regensburg

Riedenburg
Burg Rosenburg
Befreiungshalle Kelheim
Kelheim

3

Eichstätt
Willibaldsburg

Burg Prunn

93

Schloss Neuburg
Neuburg
an der Donau

92

Landshut
Stadtresidenz Landshut

Dillingen
Schloss Höchstädt

9

Burg Trausnitz

Neu-Ulm

8

Augsburg

Schloss Dachau

Schloss Lustheim
Schloss Schleißheim

Englischer Garten

Burg Burghausen

7

Schloss Nymphenburg
Residenz München

Ruhmeshalle und Bavaria

München

96 Künstlerhaus Gasteiger
Ammersee

Chiem-
see
Schloss Herrenchiemsee

Roseninsel Park Feldafing
Starnberger
See

Residenz Kempten
Kempten

Staffel-
see

Forggen-
see

95

Tegern-
see

8

93

Künstlerhaus Exter

Bodensee
Lindau

Schloss Linderhof
Ettal

Garmisch-Partenkirchen

St. Bartholomä
Königs-
see

Schloss Neuschwanstein
Füssen

Königshaus am Schachen

Bayreuth/ ■ Sanspareil
Wonsees   Rock Garden and Oriental Building
Rococo rooms, garden parterre and Rock Garden
TEL. (0 92 74) 80 89 09 - 11 · **FAX** (0 92 74) 80 89 09 - 15

■ **Zwernitz Castle** Castle complex; Permanent exhibition »Hunting in the time of the margraves«

Burghausen ■ Burghausen Castle
Castle complex, ducal apartments, chapel, State Gallery of Old German Masters and Historical Paintings, viewing platform
TEL. (0 86 77) 46 59 · **FAX** (0 86 77) 6 56 74

Cadolzburg ■ Castle and Castle Garden
TEL. (09 11) 24 46 59 - 0 · **FAX** (09 11) 24 46 59 - 300

Coburg ■ Ehrenburg Palace
Historical residential and state rooms from the Baroque era and the 19th century
TEL. (0 95 61) 80 88 - 32 · **FAX** (0 95 61) 80 88 - 31

Coburg/ ■ Rosenau Palace
Rödental   Set in an English landscape garden; residential rooms from the Biedermeier period and neo-Gothic Marble Hall
TEL. (0 95 63) 30 84 - 10 · **FAX** (0 95 63) 30 84 - 29

Dachau ■ Dachau Palace
Hall, staircase, Court Garden
TEL. (0 81 31) 8 79 23 · **FAX** (0 81 31) 7 85 73

Eichstätt ■ Willibaldsburg
Fortress complex, Jura Museum, Prehistoric and Early History Museum, Bastion Garden
TEL. (0 84 21) 47 30 · **FAX** (0 84 21) 81 94

Ellingen ■ Ellingen Residence
The state apartments of Prince von Wrede, rooms of the Deutscher Orden, palace church, historical park
TEL. (0 91 41) 9 74 79 - 0 · **FAX** (0 91 41) 9 74 79 - 7

Feldafing ■ Feldafing Park and Rose Island
Lake Starnberg   **TEL.** (0 81 51) 69 75 · **FAX** (0 81 51) 36 81 23

Herrenchiemsee ■ Herrenchiemsee New Palace
Residential and state rooms, historical gardens with waterworks and **King Ludwig II Museum**
TEL. (0 80 51) 68 87 - 0 · **FAX** (0 80 51) 68 87 - 99

94

■ **Museum in the Augustinian monastery Herrenchiemsee (Old Palace)**
Permanent exhibition on the former monastery and the constitutional convention, apartment of King Ludwig II; State Rooms in the Princes' tract; Julius Exter Art Gallery; Maler am Chiemsee Gallery

Höchstädt ■ **Höchstädt Palace**
Exhibition on the Battle of Höchstädt/Blenheim 1704, Chapel, Museum of German Faience
TEL. (0 90 74) 9 58 57 12 · **FAX** (0 90 74) 9 58 57 91

Holzhausen ■ **Gasteiger House**
Collection of Anna and Mathias Gasteiger's works in the rooms of the summer villa where they lived, landscape garden
TEL. (0 88 06) 6 99

Kelheim ■ **Hall of Liberation**
Neoclassical memorial, impressive domed hall, view of the surroundings from the open gallery
TEL. (0 94 41) 6 82 07-10 · **FAX** (0 94 41) 6 82 07-20

Kempten ■ **Kempten Residence**
State rooms and Throne Room of the prince-abbots
TEL. (08 31) 2 56-2 51 · **FAX** (08 31) 2 56-2 60

Königssee ■ **St Bartholomä**
Church St. Bartholomä, hunting lodge, chapel of St Johann and St Paul, Berchtesgaden national park
TEL. (0 80 51) 9 66 58-0 · **FAX** (0 80 51) 9 66 58-38

Kulmbach ■ **Plassenburg**
Schöner Hof (Beautiful Courtyard), Hohenzollern Museum, »Frederick the Great« Army Museum
TEL. (0 92 21) 82 20-0 · **FAX** (0 92 21) 82 20-26

Landshut ■ **Trausnitz Castle**
Castle complex, medieval halls and castle chapel, Fools' Staircase, Renaissance rooms, Museum of Renaissance Art
TEL. (08 71) 9 24 11-0/-44 · **FAX** (08 71) 9 24 11-40

■ **Town Residence**
Arcaded courtyard, First palace in Italian Renaissance style north of the alps, chapel, Neoclassical Birkenfeld Rooms

Lauenstein ■ **Lauenstein Castle**
near Ludwigsstadt Castle complex, residential rooms, special museum collections
TEL. (0 92 63) 4 00 · **FAX** (0 92 63) 97 44 22

Linderhof ■ **Linderhof Palace**
Residential and state rooms, Venus Grotto, Moroccan House, Moorish Kiosk,
Hunding's Hut and the Hermitage of Gurnemanz, historic gardens with waterwo
TEL. (0 88 22) 92 03 - 0 · **FAX** (0 88 22) 92 03 - 11

Munich ■ **Munich Residence and Court Garden**
Historical residential and state rooms representing a range of epochs
from the Renaissance to the 19th century, court church and chapel,
special collections (silver, porcelain, sacred vestments, reliquaries)
TEL. (0 89) 2 90 67 - 1 · **FAX** (0 89) 2 90 67 - 2 25

Treasury of the Residence
Cuvilliés Theatre

■ **Feldherrnhalle (Field Marshals' Hall)**

■ **Hall of Fame and statue of Bavaria** on the Theresienhöhe

■ **Nymphenburg Palace**
State rooms, Great Hall, Gallery of Beauties, palace chapel
TEL. (0 89) 1 79 08 - 0 · **FAX** (0 89) 1 79 08 - 6 27

Amalienburg, Badenburg, Pagodenburg, Magdalenenklause
in the historical palace park

Marstallmuseum
Court carriages and sleighs, saddles and other riding equipment

Museum of Nymphenburg Porcelain Bäuml Collection

■ **English Garden** Landscape garden in the English style
TEL. (0 89) 3 86 66 39 - 0 · **FAX** (0 89) 3 86 66 39 - 23

Munich/ ■ **Schleißheim New Palace**
Oberschleißheim Halls, state apartments, State Gallery of European Baroque Art,
Baroque Court Garden
TEL. (0 89) 31 58 72 - 0 · **FAX** (0 89) 31 58 72 - 50

■ **Lustheim Palace** Museum of Meißen Porcelain, hall

Neuburg ■ **Neuburg Palace on the Danube**
a.d. Donau Sgraffito façade, 1st Protestant chapel, grottoes, Pfalz-Neuburg Museum, Mus
of Baroque sacred art, Museum of Archaeology, State Gallery of Flemish Art
TEL. (0 84 31) 64 43 - 0 · **FAX** (0 84 31) 64 43 - 44

Neuschwanstein ■ **Neuschwanstein Castle**
/Schwangau Royal apartments and state rooms
TEL. (0 83 62) 9 39 88 - 0 · **FAX** (0 83 62) 9 39 88 - 18

Nuremberg ■ **Imperial Castle of Nuremberg**
Palas, period rooms, double chapel, Deep Well and Sinwell Tower,
Castle Gardens
TEL. (09 11) 24 46 59 - 0 · **FAX** (09 11) 24 46 59 - 300

Prunn ■ **Prunn Castle**
im Altmühltal Historical castle rooms, chapel
TEL. (0 94 42) 33 23 · **FAX** (0 94 42) 33 35

Riedenburg ■ **Rosenburg Castle**
Castle complex with a privately run falconry
TEL. (0 94 42) 27 52 · **FAX** (0 94 42) 32 87

Schachen ■ **King's House on the Schachen**
Residential rooms and Turkish Hall, alpine garden
TEL. (0 88 22) 92 03 - 0 · **FAX** (0 88 22) 92 03 - 11

Schnaittach ■ **Rothenburg Fortress**
The ruins of an 18th-century fortress complex
TEL./FAX (0 91 53) 80 87

Übersee/ ■ **Exter House**
Feldwies With the atelier of the artist Julius Exter
TEL. (0 86 42) 89 50 - 83 · **FAX** (0 86 42) 89 50 - 85

Veitshöchheim ■ **Veitshöchheim Palace and Court Garden**
Historical residential rooms,
Exhibition on the history of the Court Garden,
Rococo Garden with waterworks
TEL. (09 31) 9 15 82

Wonsees ■ **See Bayreuth**

Würzburg ■ **Würzburg Residence**
Baroque state rooms, frescos by G.B. Tiepolo, art gallery,
Court Gardens
TEL. (09 31) 3 55 17 - 0 · **FAX** (09 31) 3 55 17 - 25

■ **Marienburg Fortress**
Fortress complex, Prince's Building Museum with Treasury,
Sacred Vestment Room and municipal history collections,
Maschikuli Tower, Prince's Garden, Main-Franconian Museum

THE PUBLICATIONS OF THE BAVARIAN
PALACE DEPARTMENT

The Bavarian Palace Department publishes official guides with colour photos on all the places of interest for which it is responsible; a number of these are available in several languages. It also offers plans of many of the parks accompanied by brief, illustrated descriptions. Exhibition catalogues and inventories, picture books and scientific works complete the varied spectrum of publications. In addition to the books there are also posters and CD-ROMs on individual properties and special topics.

A complete list of publications can be ordered free of charge from the following address:

 Bayerische Verwaltung der
staatlichen Schlösser, Gärten und Seen

Postfach 20 20 63 · 80020 München
Tel. (0 89) 1 79 08-0 · Fax (0 89) 1 79 08-190
online-bookshop: www.schloesser.bayern.de

INFORMATION

OFFICIAL GUIDES

Published in German; some also available in English, French, Italian, Spanish and Japanese

Ansbach	Residenz Ansbach
Aschaffenburg	Aschaffenburg Castle and Pompeiianum; Schloss und Park Schönbusch
Bamberg/Memmelsdorf	Neue Residenz Bamberg (with English summary); Seehof Palace and Park
Bayreuth	The Hermitage at Bayreuth; Margravial Opera House Bayreuth (with English summary), Neues Schloss Bayreuth
Bayreuth/Wonsees	Felsengarten Sanspareil; Burg Zwernitz (with English summary)
Burghausen	Burg zu Burghausen (with English summary)
Coburg	Coburg Ehrenburg Palace
Coburg/Rödental	Schloss Rosenau (with English summary)
Dachau	Schloss Dachau
Eichstätt	Willibaldsburg Eichstätt
Ellingen	Residenz Ellingen
Feldafing	Die Roseninsel im Starnberger See
Herrenchiemsee	Augustinian Monastery and New Palace of Herrenchiemsee
Kelheim	Kelheim Hall of Liberation
Königssee	St. Bartholomä am Königssee (with English summary)
Kulmbach	Plassenburg ob Kulmbach
Landshut	Landshut Burg Trausnitz; Stadtresidenz Landshut
Lauenstein b. Ludwigsstadt	Burg Lauenstein
Linderhof	Linderhof Palace
Munich	Residence Munich; The Treasury in the Munich Residence; Altes Residenztheater/Cuvilliés-Theater; Englischer Garten München (with English summary); Ruhmeshalle und Bavaria; Nymphenburg, Palace, Park and Pavilions; Marstallmuseum Schloss Nymphenburg
Neuburg a.d. Donau	Schloss Neuburg a.d. Donau (with English summary)
Neuschwanstein	Neuschwanstein Castle
Nuremberg	Imperial Castle Nuremberg
Oberschleißheim	Schloss Schleißheim, Neues Schloss und Garten (with English summary)
Prunn	Burg Prunn
Riedenburg	Burg Rosenburg in Riedenburg an der Altmühl
Schachen	The Royal House on the Schachen
Veitshöchheim	Schloss Veitshöchheim und Hofgarten
Würzburg	Festung Marienberg zu Würzburg; The Würzburg Residence and Court Gardens

The present edition of the Official Guide to Neuschwanstein was revised by Uwe Gerd Schatz and Friederike Ulrichs. It is based on the 1933 edition of the Neuschwanstein Official Guide, written by Heinrich Kreisel, expanded by Hans Thoma and subsequently revised by Michael Petzet, Gerhard Hojer and Horst Stierhof, with further revision by Elmar D. Schmid in 1991.

Picture credits: Bayerisches Hauptstaatsarchiv, Abteilung 3, Geheimes Hausarchiv, Kabinettsakten König Maximilian II. 12 p.: p. 8–9 • Josef Beck, Eschenlohe: cover • Diderot Verlag, Rottenburg: p. 76 • Peter Frese, München: p. 80 • Kienberger, Lechbruck: p. 48, 72 • Metz, Tübingen: p. 47, 52–53, 68 • Nationalarchiv der Richard-Wagner-Stiftung, Bayreuth: p. 12 • Neumeister, München: p. 54 • Schöning & Co., Lübeck: p. 24–25, 44–45, 60, 78 • Wartburg-Stiftung, Eisenach: p. 33
All others: Bayerische Schlösserverwaltung/Rainer Herrmann/Ulrich Pfeuffer/Maria Scherf etc

Index of artists and craftsmen: Irmgard Killing

3rd edition of the new version
© Bayerische Verwaltung der staatlichen Schlösser, Gärten und Seen, München 2011
Project manager: Kathrin Jung
Translated by Sue Bollans
Edited by Irmgard Killing
Graphic design: Verena Fleischmann, Munich
Lithography: Reproline Genceller, Munich
Printed by Mediahaus Biering GmbH, Munich
ISBN 978-3-941637-08-5
Printed in Germany